Panther and Gazelle

Panther and Gazelle

Poems by Paula Ludwig

Translated by
Martina Thomson

HEARING EYE

Published by Hearing Eye 2012

Hearing Eye, Box 1, 99 Torriano Avenue, London NW5 2RX, UK

email: hearing_eye@torriano.org

www.hearingeye.org

ISBN: 978-1-905082-67-4

I am indebted to Heide Helwig for her biography,
'Ob niemand mich ruft' Das Leben der Paula Ludwig
(Langewiesche-Brandt KG)

With warm thanks to Susan Johns for her sensitive and
inspired editorial guidance. – *Martina Thomson*

Book design: Wordsmith Design
Printed by: Catford Print Centre
Distribution: Central Books, 99 Wallis Road, London E9 5LN
Representation: Inpress Ltd, www.inpressbooks.co.uk

Autograph poems

Introduction

Paula Ludwig was born in 1900 in Vorarlberg in Austria.
'I was born,' she writes 'under a full moon in a castle in the middle of a wood.' The castle was small and a bit of a ruin where her parents, who were poor, lived rent free. Her father, a carpenter, had worked for a firm that made organ screens. He now made coffins. Her mother was a seamstress.

Paula's early childhood was extremely happy with the freedom of the woods and the village, with Saints' Days and animals, but when she was five her parents split up and life for her mother became a struggle. Yet Paula did well at her convent school where she started writing poems. She always regretted her lack of further education.

When Paula was fourteen her mother died. She and her siblings joined their father in what was then Breslau in Germany, and she was forced to go into domestic service. After two years, 'by a lucky star' she found her way to the Breslau Art School where she became maid of all work, posed as a model and, importantly, learned to paint. She loved the new ambiance and it led, a little later, to her discovery of the Breslau Poetry School where a group of poets met to read and discuss their poems. Paula became a very active member.

In 1916 Paula gave birth to a child. Deserted by its father she hid away in a small village and supported herself by peddling shoelaces. Later too, with her son, she just managed to keep afloat, often by selling her small, dreamlike watercolours; at times she took refuge in charitable Mothers' Homes. Towards the end of the Great War, in 1918, she

made her way to Munich where she moved among actors, painters and poets and where her first slim book of lyrics *Die Selige Spur (A Trace of Bliss)* was published in 1920.

In 1923 she arrived in Berlin, then a lively centre for the arts. 'If only one didn't have to eat!' she said. Paula worked away at her painting, then closed her paint-box and returned to poetry after a gap of five years. *Der Himmlische Spiegel (The Heavenly Mirror)* was published in 1927, soon followed by a second edition.

It was in 1931 that Paula met the poet Iwan (Yvan) Goll who became the great love of her life. He is the 'Dark God' to whom her third collection *Dem Dunklen Gott* (1932) is dedicated. 'It's my testament' she declared. 'By fate a Jew, by accident born in France, on paper a German', that's how Goll described himself. He lived in Paris and moved among the surrealist poets and painters who were prominent in the nineteen twenties and thirties. His fame rests largely on his poem cycle *Jean Sans Terre* (John Landless – a sort of Everyman figure), to which he added over the years. As he moved between countries and languages, as he wrote in both French and German, he also moved between Paula in Germany and his wife in Paris. Absence, expectation and the foretaste of parting are reflected throughout Paula's book.

In answer, or as an echo maybe, to Paula's Dark God, Goll composed a cycle of short poems, *Chansons Malaises* (Malayan Songs: Manyana sings). In October 1934 Goll asked Paula to make two or three drawings for his book, of Manyana the singer, 'more girl than man'. She produced 55 brush drawings at one go. Two of these are reproduced here.

Meanwhile Hitler was gaining power in Germany. When some of her friends became Nazis, Paula began a retreat from Berlin by accepting an invitation to join a friend in Ehrwald, a village in the Austrian Tyrol, where with minimal living costs she could write and paint. Giving herself to her own work, she felt, was in itself a resistance to the political situation.

My parents, both from Vienna, lived in Berlin and, before finally settling in Ehrwald, Paula was often at home in our house. My memory of Paula Ludwig is from that time. She was very beautiful and not quite like a grown-up. When her coffee was too hot, she spilt it in her saucer to drink. Her voice had a lovely Austrian lilt and she coined a phrase which took root in our family: it was that she often needed a little 'movement money', 'Bewegungsgeld'.

She was, I think, especially close to my father. Her books, with dedications to him, are now on my shelves and in them she would often write out some of her poems, even some like 'On the Death of a Friend', that may never have been published. Three of these poems in manuscript are reproduced here.

Emigration would have been the great topic among people threatened by, or simply against, the incoming regime. Goll told Paula, who had plans to go to Brazil: 'For a German poet like you to breathe and sing you need the earth and sky that gave you your language. You can live anywhere but your poetry can't.' There was the alternative of an 'inner emigration', to stay and live as part of a small subversive minority, attempting to keep the German language and culture alive.

Hitler came to power in 1933. In 1938 he marched into Austria. Paula, in sympathy with her Jewish friends, and to help her son avoid fighting in the German army, left for Paris and eventually, fleeing across the Pyrenees, reached Brazil.

After thirteen isolated and financially hard years there, Paula returned to Germany where she heard that Goll had died. Some old friends, including Berthold Brecht, tried to help her but she no longer felt able to write, she'd become an alcoholic

and the poems she did write were lengthy, heavily rhymed and had lost tautness. She was however given the Georg Trakl Prize in 1962 and, two years before her death, a special prize in Vienna for her overall achievement, which includes her two prose books written in Ehrwald, a book of dreams, *Trumlandschaft* (1935) and an account of her childhood, *Buch des Lebens* (1936). It occasioned a wonderful last expedition with her son in his yellow sports car, 'just like a brimstone butterfly'.

She died in 1974.

42 poems from
To the Dark God

Dem Dunklen Gott:
Ein Jahresgedicht der Liebe
1932

The Dark God

He came from afar
and alas returned to faraway lands.

Shadows of the mountains of death
preceded him, night-birds shrieked,
and oh, how large and high the Southern Cross
climbed above my head.

But once he was here the world was full of sweetness;
the lovely scent of his body wafted ahead of him
and made our country roses blush.
Silky flowers lowered their heads
before the girlish grace of the man.

Out of the midnight of his being he rose,
radiant,
a black diamond,
a king in his splendour.

I became a dancer under his eyes –
darkly his voice beat the gong of my heart.
Under his hands
the iris of my body blossomed.

He leapt at me with the blackness of a panther,
in the skin of a deer he lay at my side.

He drank my eyes as if they were grapes,
ate my heart like a wild fruit,
hurled my soul into the universe,
storm-petrel that finds no way home.

My skies were light
but his shadow has taken them all.

He strewed star seeds on my flowerbeds
yet monsters have sprung from them
that suck my blood and grow huge.

The earth no longer holds poisons for me,
I drank the strongest from his lips.

I gave myself to his beating wings
not knowing where the flight would end –

But now I need not fear death
for darker than death is the one I love.

Who told you where I was
– have I even got a name?
Wasn't I well hidden in the bushes,
buried in brown leaves,
overhung by green branches?
Weren't my eyes swamped in mud,
my toes entangled in softwood roots?

And yet, you found my trail.
With the nose of a hunter
– no sling or knife –
you stalked me on shadowed paths,
with an eye one cannot see
you saw me.

In this blackness I gave myself away –
not a leaf stirred,
not a drop fell –
but in the silence you heard
my hands growing towards you.

Alas I fell
into a rosebush.

Now I don't know
what keeps me prisoner:

Is it the delicate thorns
or the wild scent of the roses.

You borrowed your head from the yellow roses
the way it tilts
all drawn down by kisses.

When you return it's always
as though I saw you
for the first time:

my soul emits a silver dust
as catkins do
when Spring winds first touch them.

The midnight star has risen
all other stars have gone
the wind no longer blows
the animals have ceased to breathe.
My body now is nothing but an eye
that gazes up at an unbounded sky
into its single star.

In the evening the pink hyacinth
began to send out a sweet smell
and unstoppably her soul flowed out of her.

It never returned to the faded flower.

But who minded that?

We remember her with rapture
merely to say
how unforgettably sweet
the scent of the pink hyacinth
was that evening.

Flowering almond tree
how gently your buds began
to light up my dark rooms,
but now that you froth so in white
the whole place is holding its breath
for fear
of the first drooping blossom.

However timidly the bud
sprang open with the first
breath of day,

oh, it unfolded itself utterly
in midday's kiss.

But bare of petals
by the evening,
how stark the pistil
towers, shuddering,
in the expanse of night.

Don't look for me friends –
radiant as I was yesterday
today I'm like the cloth
with which we cover the dead.

When you left
I stayed behind as shadows
of the summer sky.

The golden lakes
no longer mirror my image.

The boundless world
has shrunk to the hem of my dress
that falls sadly from my shoulders.

My dear feet
look at me – two carrier-pigeons
deprived of their message.

So you forsook my sails
still full of your breath,
heavenly wind.

Though even my sorrow for you,
even that, still widens my sombre wings
with pride.

Loneliness already climbs
high around me –
a white wall.

Yet there's a flood by my loins,
dark as blood.
Am I drifting towards a dreamlike goal?

Or am I only a ghost ship now,
to be becalmed
at the moment
of my greatest sea adventure?

Who catches a wild dove,
tames it,
and throws it back
into skies now alien?

Oh you –
why must you now deprive me
of the dark folds of your hands.

You tempted me with sweet seeds,
taught me how to pick them from your lips.
Nestled in your warmth
I forgot the red falcon.

Cruel now the glaring light of freedom.
Take pity,
throw your loving shadow over me again,
fold my wings against your shoulder,
bed me down once more in your heart.

You came to me
wrapped in the rose colours of evening,
furtively left night's portals open behind you.

The tired flowers lifted their heads again
and smiled at you.

Now the black berries of my death ripen in your hand.

Were you not as if made of gold
when you loved me –
no rust would gnaw at you.

Fallen columns rose up
where we walked,
biblical doves flew through the room
as we kissed.

Shadows of the first beings
reached high behind us
as we stood together.

Oh, your eyes were letters of eternity,
in blissful hours I broke their seal.

I am like the panther
when she wakes from her sleep
and finds her mate gone.

She runs back and forth
on the riverbank
till the sun goes down.

And the dark of night
only widens
the sadness of her eyes.

Never has the rock-face
blazed as red as now
the sun goes down.

Above the darkest peaks
how lonely the last breath
of pink clouds.

But hours later a brilliance
breaks through once more,
white, from inside the rock –

ghost-like now –
and far from its source
fills clefts and crevices

till it too will fade
and night comes irrevocably
and the mountains sink away.

Don't bring me farewell presents.
How could I hold them
in my hands

other than the farmer holds the golden fruit
he picked up from the ground
where lightening felled
his most glorious tree.

Did I not hold you high as the mountain
does the edelweiss on its brow,

and embed you deep in my lap
as the sea its most rosy starfish?

Did I not carry you like a spell in my ear,
sweetly entwined in my flesh

and wound round my shoulders,
a magic shawl knotted three times?

Oh, I held you:
as a child holds flowers
clenched tight in tiny fists,
and loses them all.

I keep listening:
does no one call me?

Like a window
with rain
ceaselessly running down,
my face lies
under tears.

When the cold is too great
even they,
the patient birds,
cry out
before their heart stops beating.

A god exalted me
but has debased me more.

He brought me plants from heaven
to grow in my garden,
but when they were big
he pulled them up
and with them
all my homely rue and mignonette.

He carried me like a bowlful of gold-water
in lonely hands
up to his heights,
where he bathed his tired eyes
in my radiant look.
But when they were well again
he threw a stone into my open face
so that the groundwater welled up
and clouded it.

When he was cold in his desolate heavens
he fetched me as a flame from earth,
but when all his rooms were warm
he extinguished me
with his last icy breath.

Say over me once more: 'bliss'
and I'll be quiet.

But that you went
and no memory of such a sound
on your lips remains

makes me mortal.

I stayed behind
where the beach was wide
lamenting the full tide
the sea had brought me
and relentlessly taken back.

But perhaps it's only that
a life's not long enough
to await its return.

Where is the friend
who looks for my footprints
in flower-gardens,
where the gate –
which, oh,
I forgot to close as I went –
sighs in the wind.

The wildest flower of the wilderness
smiled at me.

The darkest tresses of night
slept by me:

O let me never forget
how beautiful it was

when sorrow throws its shadow
over what is no longer there.

How terribly you'll miss me, God,
when I'm no longer
the food of your heart.

You'll dig up your acres of cornfields
searching solely for me.

You'll rummage your heavens
hoping to find my eyes.

You'll dash to pieces
the precious vessel of your solitude
but I shall not be there.

For I will hide myself
where you will not find me.

I will bed down in filth,
cover myself in carrion,
in slime if must be.

O your eyes
when they spy me nowhere,
O your hands
when they reach me nowhere,

O your mouth
as it calls and calls me
for eternities
in vain.

I only play the flute
and only five notes.

When I lift it to my lips
the caravans return
and birds in dark flocks.

The fishermen row to the shore
and the scented evening draws in
back from the East.

Shadowed by ivy
I lean against the plane tree
and blow out my song for you.

Oh
How I keep wanting to speak of you,
reveal all your sweetness –

Always my lips will open
but the word
blows, like a flame, away from my mouth.

You took everything
in the frenzy of your love,
tore it away with you as you went
still on fire from the fire of our feast.

All my dances are now buried in your knees.

My scents imbue your hair,
the year's kisses linger in your mouth.

I squat, a cricket
in a stubble field,
and cry out my song,
the one thing you left me,
in a deserted land.

The God and the Dancer

I no longer miss the flowers
of the outer gardens –
they smell of death.

The ones you give me
are more beautiful,
all made of light,
the soul's lotus.

They fall from your hands,
slip without sound
from your lap,
as I dance before you
in the moonlit temple.

You stand unmoving,
dark and distant,
and look down on me.

But on quiet afternoons
in the rosy stillness
when blackbirds sing
and your dancer sleeps

you descend
and place your golden feet
in my footprints –

through closed eyes
I see you walking there
and in the numbness of sleep
feel the flutter of your hem.

When from deep dances and devotions
she gazed into the god's
unmoving face,

it so hurt her eyelids
that she staggered
through the open temple gates,
leaned against the golden trellis,
gave her forehead
to the mild wind
of the passing afternoon.

Over on the marrow path
a young man walked. He came
from his field, carried fruit
on his rounded shoulder.

He saw her standing there –
so slight a figure –

and with his brown eyes
gently smiled across,
his lips opening like dark petals
of a flower.

She watched him as he made his way
down to the nearby village

and for the first time felt a longing
to go down there like him
and rest
in the blue smoke of those quiet huts.

Panther and Gazelle

Since he came close to her that day
and she escaped –
how long, oh,
shaking in the dark pit
before she found her way back to the herd –

since then there stood a strange glow in her eyes,
new breath flew from her nostrils.

Now she no longer ran to drink –
his image glowered from the water,
nor, as before, did she step out to graze –
his shadow frightened her in every bush.
In every flower she saw his trail

as though she searched for him.

Oh, like a shudder he squatted on her neck,
like constant trembling he inhabited her flanks,
fierce pounding in her breast.

It was he who made her agile turns more agile,
stretched her narrow back more pliantly;
all her leaps were practice just for him.

When he then really came,
when, hidden in lianas, his eyes looked out at her –

she sank without a sound onto her nimble knees
and was already dead
before his paw struck down.

Now that I love you
I stand before my image in the mirror
as before the lioness in her cage:

she looks at me with her grave eyes,
looks through me far into the distance.

Eyes of love
no longer see themselves.

When you went away
further than the dead
and I didn't know
what the house was like
where you stayed
nor saw the streets
you walked down
the trees, the fences
you passed,

I no longer held on to the earth
piteously living on ash
like the nettle,

I wrenched myself free
and sprouted wings.

And like an eagle hovering
with outstretched arms
over the choicest
sweetmeats of his heart,

wide-winged I spanned the world,
high above death –

But now you've come back
how I fold my immeasurable wings
how I become a plant again
and quietly flower at your lips.

October looks at me with golden eyes
as the rounded fruit nestles
with barely a sound into yellow grass.

Oh, if I could as mildly
offer up the year's love to decay,

let it fall, radiant as maple leaves
gently rustling down to rot.

Flee then as long as day lasts.
Take with you the fruit you've harvested
but leave the one that shimmers green
deep in the branches
though it's the one
that draws your heart most tenderly,
that so disquiets your soul.
A dark law will not let you pluck it.
The noblest ones are ripening – not for us –
they are our sacrifice for the fullness of the few
which overfilled our need,
maybe a pledge towards a distant Spring.

So let them be and turn
your mouth to earthly dishes.

Soon all will be bleak around us,
already there's the piping of the wind,
already there's November
shuddering behind bushes.

For long I wouldn't grasp
this cold was real.

Now that I feel it
it's too late –

My hands no longer hold off the North wind,
my heart has lost its way to warmth,
and in this frosted night I stray alone:

One who gave refuge to the flame
finds no way home to quiet hearths.

Alone in the long night
of the North,
he yearns for the sun,

no longer believes
it will return
buries himself ever deeper in snow
stops counting the days –

but then
suddenly
something wakes him in the night:
staggering to the door
he sees it rise –

sees the sun rise –
falls to his knees and weeps.

Still I dragged along
those tears that clung to me
and the avenue of past days
reached for me with waving arms.

But in a minute I was up with the wind
that no longer touched the treetops.

Nothing is sweet to me on my return
the flowers by the wayside are sombre,
I can no longer tell them by their scent.

Oh, that some scurrying creature
would startle my indifferent heart.

Perhaps you too, cause of my poor wanderings,
are alien to me now
like the blossoming face of my homeland –

a carpet for my feet
over which I step,
after the law of clouds –
casting a shadow
but no longer touching it.

A day and a night it took me
to grasp it was you
who called me.

I trembled with the touch of your breath –
frailer than the graveyard crocus
in spring winds.

The burial-linen is still about me
the shock of resurrection in my limbs
my breasts pointed from the touch of angels.

Oh, hold me gently
softly restore my eyes.
In the darkness of your breath
let me slowly wake to life.

I was braced and big –
like a mountain range
my sorrows outgrew me.

But now I am weak.
Frightened, dumb,
I stare at the face of redemption.

Three autograph poems
with translations

'In der Allee' and 'An die Nacht' were printed in
Der Himmlische Spiegel, 1927

'Zum Tod eines Freundes' is an uncollected poem,
c. 1927

In der Allee

Als ich allein
die Allee entlang ging
das gelbe Laub über mir
langsam von den Zweigen sich löste
und ich
alles Wissen von dir
abfallen ließ
in Duft und Regen des Herbstes
dich vergaß,
am Ende des Weges
auf einmal
wieder erwachte
da war mir
als wäre ich
zutiefst in dir
trunken
diese Allee rauschender Bäume
hinabgeschritten

In der Allee

Als ich allein
die Allee entlang ging
das gelbe Laub über mir
langsam von den Zweigen sich löste
und ich
alles Wissen von dir
abfallen liess
im Duft und Regen des Herbstes
dich vergass
am Ende des Weges
auf einmal
wieder erwachte
da war mir
als wäre ich
zutiefst in dir
trunken
diese Allee rauschender Baüme
hinabgeschritten

In the Avenue

As I walked alone
along the avenue,
yellow leaves above me
slowly loosed themselves from branches
and I let go all thoughts of you,
forgot you
in the fragrance and rain of autumn....
coming to the end
I suddenly awoke –
it seemed to me I'd been
immersed in you and drunk
all the way down this avenue
of swaying trees

An die Nacht.

Ach,
noch bedrängst du mich
mit zu viel Dunkel
Nacht,
daß ich dich ganz begreife,
aber wenn der Tag beginnt
dann erscheinst du mir herrlich
und in der Erinnerung
wächst mir dein Wesen ganz in den
                                    Schoß.

Ich verlange den Abend
und deine Wiederkehr
süßeste Freundin.

60

An die Nacht

Ach,
noch bedrängst du mich
mit zuviel Dunkel
Nacht,
dass ich dich ganz begreife,
aber wenn der Tag beginnt
dann erscheinst du mir herrlich,
und in der Erinnerung
wächst mir dein Wesen ganz in den Schoss.

Ich verlange den Abend
und deine Wiederkehr
süsseste Freundin.

To the Night

You overawe me still,
oh night,
with too much darkness
for me to fully grasp you.
But as day begins
you seem magnificent –
and when recalled
your being settles in my lap.

I yearn for evening
and for your return,
sweetest friend.

(Zum Tod eines Freundes)

Von alten Wäldern her ein Wind gesendet
daß sich das Blatt das fällt
auf das verfallne lege
und tief die Kühle dieses Tals sich rege
da eines Vogels schöner Flug sich wendet

———

Zum Tod eines Freundes

Von alten Wäldern her ein Wind gesendet
dass sich das Blatt das fällt
auf das verfallne lege
und tief die Kühle dieses Tals sich rege
da eines Vogels schöner Flug sich wendet

For the Death of a Friend

Across old woods a wind is sent
to place the falling leaf
on one already in decay
and deeply stir the coolness of this valley
as the splendid flight of a bird now turns.

About the translator

Martina Thomson was born in Berlin of Austrian parents, and came to England as a child. She is a potter, a poet and translator. Trained as an art therapist, she worked for many years in psychiatry. She came late to poetry; her work now appears in many magazines. She lives and works in Camden Town.

Her previous books are
On Art and Therapy (Virago, 1989, 1991)
Ferryboats (Torriano Poetry Pamphlet, N° 54. Hearing Eye, 2008)

Watercolour by Paula Ludwig: *Children in a Berlin garden.*
(Martina and her brother Thomas)